MONSTER LAW

REAL LAWS ABOUT MONSTERS IN AMERICA

FRANCISCO ARBENZ

Edited by
ELIJAH SULLIVAN

HANGAR 1 PUBLISHING

ACKNOWLEDGMENTS

This book is dedicated to all those with open and curious minds.

Special thanks to everyone who made this book possible, including the staff of various counties, villages, and towns mentioned, and to Mr. Jeff Wamsley, curator of the Mothman Museum in Point Pleasant, West Virginia, and above all my beautiful fiancé.

A NOTE ON NAMES AND TERMS

Although the terms "Bigfoot" and "Abominable Snowman" are widely used to refer to upright, hair covered cryptids, this book will refer to them as "sasquatch" or "sasquatches" whenever possible out of deference to and respect for the Indigenous Peoples of North America. "Sasquatch" is an anglicized form of the Salish name "Sasq'ets"—meaning "wild man" or "hairy man"—and predates the use of the more popular term "Bigfoot."

CONTENTS

INTRODUCTION

As the older gentleman told his story, I listened attentively.

"It grabbed the tree branch to its left, with human fingers that disturb me more in hindsight than they did in the moment, and stared at me. That dark and hairy face, with eyes so intelligent and curious... all it did was stare."

"How long did you see it for?" I asked him.

"Only a few moments, but it felt like 10 minutes," the old, gray-bearded man answered.

"How tall was it, if you can remember?"

"Easily 8 feet, it was hidden behind some bushes, and I assumed it was standing on a rock or elevated spot, but when I returned to the same spot a few days later I found nothing it could've been standing on."

"What happened next?"

"It stared at me, and then it let go of the branch and walked away. That was ten years ago, and it is the strangest memory I have."

I glanced over at my friends, who had been listening as I had, and saw a mix of expressions on their faces that ranged from vague interest to outright skepticism. I thanked the man for his time, and we continued on through the Vermont wilderness, eyes peeled for any hairy giants that might cross our path.

Cryptozoology—the study of hidden or unknown animals, coined by biologist Ivan T. Sanderson in the 1940s—is something that has fascinated the American public for generations. Tales of sasquatches and lake monsters can make one feel there remains some adventure and mystery in our otherwise exhaustively mapped and increasingly connected world. In many instances, belief in these mysterious creatures permeates communities so deeply that some of them, as you will learn throughout this book, have adopted or implemented legislation to protect and recognize the existence of these creatures. While some scoff at such laws and ordinances, it should be understood that laws are ideally a reflection of a society's shared values. The laws mentioned in this book are examples of democracy in progress, as well as examples of the cultural impact cryptozoology has on our society. I hope you find learning about these laws as interesting as I did, and that you'll someday have the chance to visit these places where monsters roam.

1

ACTIVE LAWS & ORDINANCES

The following laws regarding monsters have been either enacted or symbolically adopted.

Skamania County, Washington

Home to Mt. St. Helens and the infamous Ape Canyon (where an alleged conflict between miners and several aggressive sasquatches played out in 1924), Skamania County was among the first in the nation to pass legislation protecting sasquatches. In 1969, a mere two years after the famous Patterson-Gimlin film (a one-minute-long recording of an alleged sasquatch) was shot, Skamania County's Board of Commissioners passed ordinance 1969-01.

Unlike other, more symbolic cryptid-related laws, this ordinance had stern enforcement mechanisms written into it which made observers take it more seriously and included making any "premeditated, willful and wanton slaying of any such creature" a felony, punishable by a fine not exceeding "ten thousand dollars and/or imprisonment in the county jail for a period not to exceed five years." In a 1971 interview with local KGW News, County Commissioner Conrad Lundy stated, "I felt, and the Board of County Commissioners felt, that we should protect this animal and also the lives of our local citizens. [With] people coming into the area with guns and shooting everything that moves, we might have a fatality." The legislative intent of the ordinance was to protect humans and sasquatches alike. Mr. Lundy continued, "We had people coming in from the outside area with high-powered rifles and every means to kill the animal," further emphasizing the need for the measure.

Nevertheless, the punishments stated in that ordinance were perceived as overly harsh by some observers, and in 1984 it was partially repealed by Ordinance No 1984-2. Drastic changes resulted, including distinguishing between sasquatch slayings based on whether or not the action was committed with malice aforethought. Should a killing of a sasquatch be done in this manner, the new ordinance would classify it as a "Gross Misdemeanor" punishable by "1 year in the county jail and a $1,000.00 fine, or both." If the slaying of a sasquatch was found not to have been carried out with malice aforethought, the ordinance would classify it as a simple misdemeanor and deem it punishable by "a $500.00 fine and up to 6 months in the county jail, or both." The ordinance also eliminated the diminished capacity, or "diseased mind" defense that any sasquatch hunter could previously have used as justification for their actions. Interestingly, the ordinance took it a step further and declared that should the sasquatch in question be determined to be more closely related to humans (or humanoid) rather than more ape-like (anthropoid), then the applicable laws used by the prosecuting attorney should be those pertaining to homicide rather than those listed in the ordinance. Clearly, this was a raising of the stakes far higher than in the previous ordinance! Lastly, the ordinance also declared sasquatches an endangered species and created a sasquatch refuge in Skamania County.

ORDINANCE NO. 1984-2

PARTIALLY REPEALING AND AMENDING ORDINANCE NO. 1969-01

WHEREAS, evidence continues to accumulate indicating the possible existence within Skamania County of a nocturnal primate mammal variously described as an ape-like creature or a sub-species of Homo Sapiens; and

WHEREAS, legend, purported recent findings, and spoor support this possibility; and

WHEREAS, this creature is generally and commonly known as "Sasquatch", "Yeti", "Bigfoot", or "Giant Hairy Ape", all of which terms may hereinafter be used interchangeably; and

WHEREAS, publicity attendant upon such real or imagined findings and other evidence have resulted in an influx of scientific investigators as well as casual hunters, most of which are armed with lethal weapons; and

WHEREAS, the absence of specific national and state laws restricting the taking of specimens has created a dangerous state of affairs within this county with regard to firearms and other deadly devices used to hunt the Yeti and poses a clear and present danger to the safety and well-being of persons living or traveling within the boundaries of this county as well as to the Giant Hairy Apes themselves; and

WHEREAS, previous County Ordinance No. 1969-01 deemed the slaying of such a creature to be a felony (punishable by 5 years in prison) and may have exceeded the jurisdictional authority of that Board of County Commissioners; now, therefore

BE IT HEREBY ORDAINED BY THE BOARD OF COUNTY COMMISSIONERS OF SKAMANIA COUNTY that that portion of Ordinance No. 1969-01, deeming the slaying of Bigfoot to be a felony and punishable by 5 years in prison, is hereby repealed and in its stead the following sections are enacted:

SECTION 1. Sasquatch Refuge. The Sasquatch, Yeti, Bigfoot, or Giant Hairy Ape are declared to be endangered species of Skamania County and there is hereby created a Sasquatch Refuge, the boundaries of which shall be co-extensive with the boundaries of Skamania County.

SECTION 2. Crime - Penalty. From and after the passage of this ordinance the premeditated, wilful, or wanton slaying of Sasquatch shall be unlawful and shall be punishable as follows:

(a) If the actor is found to be guilty of such a crime with malice aforethought, such act shall be deemed a Gross Misdemeanor.

(b) If the act is found to be premeditated and wilful or wanton but without malice aforethought, such act shall be deemed a Misdemeanor.

(c) A gross misdemeanor slaying of Sasquatch shall be punishable by 1 year in the county jail and a $1,000.00 fine, or both.

(d) The slaying of Sasquatch which is deemed a misdemeanor shall be punishable by a $500.00 fine and up to 6 months in the county jail, or both.

SECTION 3. Defense. In the prosecution and trial of any accused Sasquatch killer the fact that the actor is suffering from insane delusions, diminished capacity, or that the act was the product of a diseased mind, shall not be a defense.

SECTION 4. Humanoid/Anthropoid. Should the Skamania County Coroner determine any victim/creature to have been humanoid the Prosecuting Attorney shall persue the case under existing laws pertaining to homicide. Should the coroner determine the victim to have been an anthropoid (ape-like creature) the Prosecuting Attorney shall proceed under the terms of this ordinance.

BE IT FURTHER ORDAINED that the situation existing constitutes an emergency and as such this ordinance shall become effective immediately upon its' passage.

REVIEWED this 2nd day of April, 1984, and set for public hearing on the 16th day of April , 1984, at 10:30 o'clock A.m.

BOARD OF COUNTY COMMISSIONERS
Skamania County, Washington

_____
Chairman

_____
Commissioner

_____
Commissioner

ATTEST:
_____
County Auditor and Ex-Officio Clerk of
the Board

ORDINANCE NO. 1984-2
Page 2 of 3 Pages

4

ORDINANCE NO. *1984-02* IS HEREBY DULY PASSED AND ADOPTED
INTO LAW this *16th* day of *April*, 1984.

BOARD OF COUNTY COMMISSIONERS
Skamania County, Washington

_____
                                    Chairman

_____
                                    Commissioner

_____
                                    Commissioner

ATTEST:

_____
County Auditor and Ex-Officio Clerk
        of the Board

Whatcom County, Washington

Whatcom County is known for two things: mass production of rasp-berries, and sasquatch reports. If you find that first claim hard to believe, you should know that Whatcom County actually produces the largest per capita crop of red raspberries in the entire world. As for the second claim, according to the Bigfoot Field Researchers Organization (BFRO), there have been at least 21 sasquatch reports in Whatcom County since the 1970s. Located just south of British Columbia, Canada, Whatcom County has a long history of sasquatches that predates the arrival of European settlers. Coast Salish Natives have lived in what is now called Whatcom County for thousands of years, and the Lummi Nation and Nooksack Tribes both live there to this day. The word "sasquatch" is, in fact, an anglicized version of the Salish word "Sasq'ets" used by the Sts'ailes people to refer to the elusive creature.

In early June of 1992, Whatcom County followed in the footsteps of Skamania County by passing Resolution No. 92-043, which created a sasquatch refuge area and argued that "if such a creature exists, it is inadequately protected and in danger of death or injury." Unlike Skamania, however, Whatcom County did not sign into this law any punishments or consequences for anyone who might violate it. As a result, the law is more symbolic and amounts to little more than a sign of good faith toward and recognition of sasquatch and their impact on the culture of Whatcom County.

bigfoot.res 6/9/91

SPONSORED BY: _Consent_____

PROPOSED BY: _Harris_____

INTRODUCTION DATE: _6/9/92_____

1   RESOLUTION NO. _92-043_

2   DECLARING WHATCOM COUNTY A SASQUATCH PROTECTION

3   AND REFUGE AREA

4   WHEREAS, legend, purported recent findings and spoor suggest that Bigfoot may
5 exist; and

6   WHEREAS, if such a creature exists, it is inadequately protected and in danger of
7 death or injury;

8   NOW, THEREFORE, BE IT RESOLVED by the Whatcom County Council that,
9 Whatcom County is hereby declared a Sasquatch protection and refuge area, and all
10 citizens are asked to recognize said status.

.1   BE IT FURTHER RESOLVED, this resolution shall be effective immediately.

12   APPROVED this _9th_ day of _June___, 1991.

13   WHATCOM COUNTY COUNCIL
14 ATTEST: WHATCOM COUNTY, WASHINGTON

15
16 Ramona Reeves, Council Clerk   Daniel M. Warner, Chair

17 APPROVED AS TO FORM:

18
19 Civil Deputy Pros. Atty.

Grays Harbor & Clallam Counties, Washington

You may know it as the birthplace of famed Nirvana Guitarist, Kurt Cobain, or physicist and Nobel laureate, Dr. Douglas Dean Osheroff. Grays Harbor County is also famous in sasquatch hunting circles for a long history of sightings, including one yielding a discovery by a reputable investigator in the form of Deputy Sheriff Dennis Hereford. He and other officers were investigating a report by several loggers on the Satsop River when they found several footprints with such extensive anatomical detail that they are considered by some to be among the strongest pieces of evidence for sasquatches' existence.

In March of 2022, a class of fifth grade students from Lincoln Elementary took further steps to solidify Grays Harbor County into the sasquatch legend. As part of a class project created by their teacher, Ms. Andrews, the students wrote to the county's Board of Commissioners to express their concern for sasquatches and ask that they take action to protect the species. To their surprise, their request was taken seriously and Ordinance No. 2022-037 was passed on April 5th, 2022. The conservationist spirit of Lincoln Elementary's students is prevalent in the ordinance, as it presumes that the sasquatch population is struggling and on the verge of extinction and therefore creates a protective refuge for the species. Though the ordinance lacks any enforcement mechanism—with no fines or prison sentences listed should someone violate it by harming a sasquatch within the allotted refuge area—a student from Lincoln Elementary would later express to the Chronicle newspaper that having such a refuge for sasquatches would also provide researchers the opportunity to study them in their natural environment, should the species be verified to exist.

On April 11th, 2023, that same Lincoln Elementary classroom lobbied the Clallam Board of Commissioners to pass another sasquatch ordinance, similar to that of Grays Harbor. This latest project was born out of Ms. Andrews' "Saving Sasquatch" lesson which was geared towards teaching her students how to get involved in civics. Lincoln Elementary Principal, Kent Nixon, complimented the lesson as "a beautiful combination of language arts, science, and civics." Clallam County's proclamation "recognizes and honors" sasquatches and recognizes Clallam County as a "refuge for Sasquatch" and additionally supports the local festival "Forks Sasquatch Day" from May 26th through May 28th, 2023. At the very least, both laws will make some would-be hunters think twice before heading to Grays Harbor or Clallam Counties.

GRAYS HARBOR COUNTY RESOLUTION NO. 2022-037

A RESOLUTION of the Grays Harbor County Board of Commissioners Establishing Acknowledging the Potential Extinction and Necessity for Protection of the Sasquatch

WHEREAS, legends, sightings, research, investigation and recognition by various counties in various States support the notion that Sasquatch (aka Bigfoot, yeti and giant hairy ape) exists; and

WHEREAS, if Sasquatch exists, it is not flourishing – given the unusual event of being sighted; and

WHEREAS, since Sasquatch is not flourishing, it is likely an endangered species and subject to great harm and extinction if it continues to be unprotected.

NOW THEREFORE, BE IT HEREBY RESOLVED by the Board of Commissioners of Grays Harbor County that Grays Harbor County is hereby declared a Sasquatch protection and refuge area of which all citizens of the County are asked to recognize and honor.

ADOPTED this 5th day of April, 2022.

BOARD OF COMMISSIONERS
GRAYS HARBOR COUNTY

Jill Warne, Chair, Commissioner
District No. 1

Kevin Pine, Commissioner
District No. 2

Vickie L. Raines, Commissioner
District No. 3

ATTEST:

Wendy Chatham, Clerk of the Board

APPROVED AS TO FORM:

Deputy Prosecuting Attorney

Resolution 2022-037

-1-

\\d

APR 1 1 2023

PROCLAMATION

RECOGNIZING AND HONORING SASQUATCH

WHEREAS, legends, sightings, research, investigation and recognition by various counties in various States support the notion that Sasquatch (aka Bigfoot, yeti, and giant hairy ape) exists; and

WHEREAS, if Sasquatch exists, it is not flourishing – given the very unusual event of being sighted and it is likely an endangered species and subject to great harm and extinction if it continues to be unprotected;

WHEREAS, Clallam County desires that its citizens recognize the need to protect Sasquatch if it exists;

NOW, THEREFORE, WE THE BOARD OF CLALLAM COUNTY COMMISSIONERS hereby

Request all citizens of Clallam County recognize this County as a refuge for Sasquatch to prove both protection and security and also supports the Forks Sasquatch Day May 26th through May 28th, 2023

Signed this 11th day of April 2023

BOARD OF CLALLAM COUNTY COMMISSIONERS

_____
Mark Ozias, Chair

_____
Randy Johnson

_____
Mike French

City of Geneva, New York

The "lake trout capital of the world" to some, Seneca Lake in New York may also be home to a legendary river monster known as the Seneca Lake Monster. Spanning 38 miles in length and over 600 ft down at its maximum depth, Seneca Lake is even larger than the more famous Loch Ness in Scotland. Despite the Seneca Lake Monster not being one of the more readily recognizable cryptids, it does have the distinction of being one of the few to have legal protection. Spotted since the late 1800s, the Seneca Lake Monster is more akin to a sea serpent than a classic plesiosaur-like monster.

One famous story from 1899 tells of a steamboat navigating through Seneca Lake from which a creature was spotted. The captain rammed into it in an attempt to capture it dead or alive. After successfully ramming into the creature, the crew tried towing it back to shore before being forced to release it back into the depths in fear that its large size would drag them down with it. Although the veracity of this story was called into question at the time, sightings continued sporadically into the 20th century. It is perhaps this history of antagonizing the lake monster that partially motivated Geneva City Council to pass legislation protecting it. On August 5th, 2015, they voted 6-1 to amend the city's code to make the hunting of the Seneca Lake

Monster illegal. Chapter 206-2 of Geneva's municipal code states "hunting, trapping, or cause of harm to the serpent termed the Seneca Lake Monster or any of its descendants is prohibited." Additionally, the chapter further prohibits the "use [of] any City facility, including access points to Seneca Lake on City shorelines, to launch a hunting or trapping party aimed at killing, trapping, or injuring the Seneca Lake Monster or any of its descendants." The following chapter provides the penalty of "a fine not exceeding $250 or by imprisonment not exceeding 15 days" for anyone who violates the amendment.

City of Geneva, NY

Chapter 206

HUNTING AND TRAPPING

| § 206-1. | Hunting and trapping restrictions. | § 206-2. | Hunting or trapping of Seneca Lake Monster prohibited. |
| | | § 206-3. | Penalties for offenses. |

§ 206-1
§ 206-2. Hunting or trapping of Seneca Lake Monster prohibited. [Added 8-5-2015 by Ord. No. 8-2015¹] § 206-2

The hunting, trapping, or cause of harm to the serpent termed the Seneca Lake Monster or any of its descendants is prohibited. No person shall use any City facility, including access points to Seneca Lake on City shorelines, to launch a hunting or trapping party aimed at killing, trapping, or injuring the Seneca Lake Monster or any of its descendants. Possession of the carcass of said creatures, or of any live creature meeting this description, will be considered presumptive evidence of a violation of this section.

§ 206-2
§ 206-3. Penalties for offenses. § 206-3

A violation of any of the provisions of this chapter shall be punishable by a fine not exceeding $250 or by imprisonment not exceeding 15 days, or by both said fine and imprisonment. Each day any such violation shall continue shall constitute a separate violation.

Village of Whitehall, New York

While the Town of Whitehall prides itself on being "the birthplace of the US Navy," sasquatch enthusiasts know the Village of Whitehall, contained within it, as the "Sasquatch Capital of the East Coast." This unusual nickname stems from the rich history of sasquatch sightings in the area over the last several decades, including a high profile sighting reported by police officers in 1976 when they and other eyewitnesses described a "man-like beast" that stood over 8 feet tall and was covered with hair. With sightings continuing to this day, Whitehall has attracted the attention of several sasquatch enthusiasts including the team from the hit Animal Planet television series "Finding Bigfoot" in 2015. Over the years, the Village of Whitehall embraced the Sasquatch legend and on February 5th, 2004, the Village Board of Trustees adopted the "Dr Warren L. Cook Sasquatch/Bigfoot Protective Resolution" which protects sasquatches from any "potentially lethal abuse or annihilation by hunters or hunting parties" and declared them an endangered species in the Village of Whitehall. On June 19th, 2018, the Village took further steps to solidify the cultural importance of these creatures when their board passed yet another resolution, this time declaring the last Saturday of September "Sasquatch Appreciation Day" and "Sasquatch" the Official Animal of the Village of Whitehall.

The Dr. Warren L. Cook Sasquatch/Bigfoot Protective Resolution

WHEREAS, there is an historic, traditional history of accumulating reports of a bi-pedal, ape-like creature walking like a human in the Whitehall, New York area often referred to as "Bigfoot" or "Sasquatch", and

WHEREAS, reports of these creatures can be traced back to the Iroquois and Algonquins and are referenced clearly in the works of Samuel de Champlain and represent a consistent pattern of sightings, and

WHEREAS, the possibility of all endangered species, proven and pending scientific recognition, should be entitled to protection under both Federal and New York State laws, and

WHEREAS, publicity of these creatures could draw not only scientific scrutiny, but unwanted hunting parties with weapons that could pose a lethal threat to both creatures and area residents as well, and

WHEREAS, legislation to protect other cryptozoological creatures has been successfully passed in both Port Henry for The Lake Champlain Monsters popularly referred to as "Champ," and in Skamania County, Washington for "Bigfoot" or "Sasquatch",

NOW, THEREFORE BE IT RESOLVED BY THE VILLAGE BOARD OF TRUSTEES OF THE VILLAGE OF WHITEHALL, NEW YORK, that the Village of Whitehall adopt the following measures to ensure the safety of those creatures known as "bigfoot" or "Sasquatch" in the following two sections:

SECTION ONE: Sasquatch Safety Preserve- the creatures know as "Sasquatch" or "Bigfoot" are declared an endangered species in the Village of Whitehall, New York and are hereby protected from potentially lethal abuse or annihilation by hunters or hunting parties, and

SECTION TWO: The willful, premeditated act of killing or fatally injuring a "Sasquatch" or "Bigfoot" within the borders of the Village of Whitehall, New York is hereby prohibited.

Adopted this 5th day of February, 2004.

Proposed Village of Whitehall NY Resolution

Whereas since the 1970s Whitehall has become known for an inordinate number of Bigfoot sightings, mention of which goes back as far as the Iroquois and Algonquin and by Samuel de Champlain, and

Whereas in the 21st Century this has developed into a Whitehall Town Law protecting the Sasquatch as an endangered species along with an increasing number of Bigfoot-themed businesses, and

Whereas Whitehall is now the subject of Sasquatch movies, TV shows, books, and home to Bigfoot researchers and authors, and

Whereas Whitehall now displays four prominent Bigfoot statues and is home to an annual Bigfoot Half-Marathon and a Sasquatch Festival that draws people from 200 miles around the Northeastern U.S. and Canada, all making Whitehall a tourism destination-point for Bigfoot searchers,

Now Therefore Be It Resolved by the Village of Whitehall, New York, that the last Saturday of every September be officially known as Sasquatch Appreciation Day in Whitehall and that the Sasquatch will be the Official Animal of the Village of Whitehall, New York.

Adopted 6/19/18

New York

Quite possibly the most famous lake monster in the United States, Lake Champlain's "Champ" is the only cryptid to have legal protection granted by an entire state, at least symbolically. Champ was first spotted in 1819 by one "Captain Crum" but stories of serpents in the lake predate European settlement of the region. The Abenaki peoples native to the surrounding area believe that the Gitaskog or "great serpent" inhabits the lake.

Champ hunters like Katy Elizabeth believe the monster measures anywhere from 15 to 25 feet in length, and that there is more than one living in the lake. Ms. Elizabeth has posited that her photographs and own personal sighting of Champ's species are enough to strongly support their existence. But perhaps the most compelling piece of evidence supporting the creature's existence in Lake Champlain is the discovery of echolocation-like noises in the lake during a 2006 expedition. Most know echolocation—the ability to see using sound —to be a capability of species like bats, but whales and dolphins also utilize it. Whether the noises discovered by the research team in 2006 were misidentified as echolocation or not remains unknown.

Yet another strong piece of evidence for Champ's existence was the infamous 1966 photograph taken by Sandra Mansi. The photo, unlike other cryptozoological photos, is remarkably detailed and seems to depict a long-necked creature breaching the lake's surface. Skeptics argue it is merely a floating tree trunk, though Ms. Mansi remained adamant throughout her life that she'd witnessed and photographed the legendary Champ.

If Champ and its kind really do inhabit Lake Champlain, one thing is for certain: according to a historic plaque located at the town of Plattsburgh, NY, right on the Shore of Lake Champlain, there have been more than 300 sightings since the 1800s and it can be safely assumed that those living around Lake Champlain hold the legend in high regard. This is so much the case that Port Henry, a small hamlet in Essex County, NY—the place where old Captain Crum first spotted Champ in 1819—has nicknamed itself "The Home of Champ" and now celebrates "Champ Day" in honor of the legendary monster with a festival. In 1983, the New York State Assembly passed Resolution 112, which encouraged serious scientific research into Champ and prohibited any harm from coming to the creature. The law was never passed by the State Senate, though, thus making it a commemorative or symbolic piece of legislation. Nevertheless, the message is clear: Champ holds a prominent position in the folklore of the Empire State.

L 112 A. RYAN, HARRIS, CASALE, CONNERS—
Whereas, There are documented reports, historical accounts, and photographic evidence to substantiate the possible existence in Lake Champlain of an unidentified aquatic animal or animals described as longnecked, serpentine, or snakelike; and

Whereas, The animals of this kind have been part of the Champlain Valley folklore for over three and a half centuries, to the enjoyment of all citizens of the state; and

Whereas, These animals have been observed by many citizens of the state and others; and

Whereas, The discovery of a species of heretofore unknown animal life would be a contribution to the fund of human knowledge; and

Whereas, Recent publicity has generated considerable scientific curiosity to investigate these animals; and

Whereas, The absence of a state law to protect these unidentified unknown animals may encourage the use of force or violence, threatening their welfare and the safety of New Yorkers and people enjoying the beauty of Lake Champlain; and

Whereas, No act of violence by these animals has ever been recorded against any individual or group of people; and

Whereas, The most responsible course for the state of New York to follow would be to encourage continued collection and evaluation of scientific evidence of unexplained phenomena in Lake Champlain; now, therefore, be it

Resolved, That the possible existence of the animal commonly known as "Champ" is recognized by this state; and be it further

Resolved, That "Champ" should be protected from any willful act resulting in death, injury or harassment; and be further

Resolved, That the State of New York encourage serious scientific inquiry into the existence of any unusual animals in Lake Champlain, especially the possible existence of an animal such as the one commonly known as "Champ"; and be it further

Resolved, That citizens of New York and visitors to Lake Champlain are encouraged to report sightings of such animals or associated phenomena and photographic evidence whenever possible. En Con Com
Mar 16 Rept Ref to Rules Com Apr 18 Rept Adopted.

New York Legislative Record and Index 1983-Resolutions - Assembly L 112

2

WOULD-BE LAWS & ORDINANCES

The following laws pertaining to monsters failed to be adopted or enacted.

New Mexico

In late October 2016, scathing headlines throughout the country ran about an event held at the University of New Mexico's Gallup campus (UNM-G) that angered some and encouraged others. At the center of it all was Dr. Christopher Dyer, professor of Anthropology at UNM-G. Despite being one of few academics who openly researches sasquatches, he is far from being a mad scientist, and is actually an applied anthropologist who specializes in maritime anthropology, ecological anthropology, and community disaster resilience, as well as having led several field research teams in Asia, Africa, and Latin America. In October of 2016, Dr. Dyer held a two-day sasquatch conference at the UNM-G campus which was open to the public and free of charge. Two other scientists were a part of it, anthropologist Dr. Jeffrey Meldrum and naturalist Rob Kryder, who gave lectures on the study of sasquatches and presented audio evidence of their existence. The total cost of the conference—$7,458—was funded by the public university, which caused mild outrage in New Mexico.

State Senator George Munoz was particularly outraged, and subsequently sponsored a bill that would ban public funds from being used to hunt "fictitious creatures." The bill went as far as lumping sasquatches into the same category as "Pokémon, leprechauns, and bogeymen" and banned any public funds from being used to hunt any of the sort. Had this bill (SB: 243) become law, it would have taken effect on July 17, 2017. However, Senator Munoz's bill received little support and failed to pass into law during its legislative session. UNM-G president Dr. Robert Frank also expressed his disapproval of the event and claimed he did not have any knowledge of the conference until after it occurred. Nevertheless, Dr. Dyer remains steadfast in his defense of the conference as "the largest and most well-attended event in the history of this campus."

SENATE BILL 243

53RD LEGISLATURE - STATE OF NEW MEXICO - FIRST SESSION, 2017

INTRODUCED BY

George K. Munoz

AN ACT

RELATING TO HIGHER EDUCATION; RESTRICTING EXPENDITURES ON CERTAIN ACTIVITIES.

BE IT ENACTED BY THE LEGISLATURE OF THE STATE OF NEW MEXICO:

 SECTION 1. Section 21-1-23 NMSA 1978 (being Laws 1971, Chapter 228, Section 2) is amended to read:

 "21-1-23. STATE HIGHER EDUCATIONAL INSTITUTIONS--PUBLIC FUNDS--LIMITATION UPON PAYMENT FOR CERTAIN PURPOSES.--

 B. Public funds shall not be expended by a state higher educational institution for the purpose of looking for or catching a fictitious creature, including:

  (1) bigfoot;

  (2) sasquatch;

  (3) yeti;

  (4) abominable snowman;

  (5) Pokémon;

  (6) leprechauns; or

  (7) bogeyman."

 SECTION 2. EFFECTIVE DATE.--The effective date of the provisions of this act is July 1, 2017.

Oklahoma

While laws concerning cryptids usually pertain to ensuring their protection or the recognition of their cultural impact, Oklahoma's SB 1648 is perhaps the only proposed bill concerning their capture. The bill, introduced by Oklahoma State Representative Justin Humphrey, would have ordered the Oklahoma Wildlife Conservation Division to create regulations for hunting sasquatches, as well as create specific hunting licenses and accompanying fees.

"It will be a great way for people to enjoy our area and to have some fun," wrote Rep. Humphrey about the bill. Humphrey made it clear in a press release that the bill was meant to stimulate tourism and drive revenue to Oklahoma, and that he did not want anyone to actually kill a sasquatch should they indeed exist. It was Humphrey's intention for the state to capitalize on the widespread belief in sasquatches in Southwest Oklahoma, citing an already existing "Bigfoot Festival" in the region. Rep. Humphrey also indicated that he would like to work with state wildlife departments to ensure that the hunting licenses would only be for capturing or trapping a sasquatch, and not killing one, even though SB 1648 doesn't state this differentiation. Humphrey initially hoped to secure a $25,000 bounty for the first person to trap a sasquatch, though this plan—along with SB 1648 itself—failed to garner much support and the bill ultimately did not survive its legislative session.

```
 1                      STATE OF OKLAHOMA

 2            1st Session of the 58th Legislature (2021)

 3   HOUSE BILL 1648                  By: Humphrey

 4

 5

 6                       AS INTRODUCED

 7        An Act relating to game and fish; directing the
          Oklahoma Wildlife Conservation Commission to
 8        establish a big foot hunting season; providing for
          codification; and providing an effective date.
 9

10

11

12   BE IT ENACTED BY THE PEOPLE OF THE STATE OF OKLAHOMA:

13        SECTION 1.    NEW LAW    A new section of law to be codified

14   in the Oklahoma Statutes as Section 5-603 of Title 29, unless there

15   is created a duplication in numbering, reads as follows:

16        The Oklahoma Wildlife Conservation Commission shall promulgate

17   rules establishing a big foot hunting season.  The Commission shall

18   set annual season dates and create any necessary specific hunting

19   licenses and fees.

20        SECTION 2.  This act shall become effective November 1, 2021.

21

22        58-1-5153     AMM     01/05/21

23

24
```

Washington

With so many counties in Washington state having their own laws protecting sasquatches, one might be surprised to learn that there exists no statewide law protecting the famous cryptid. On August 26th, 1970, Washington Governor Daniel J. Evans made a symbolic proclamation that declared "all Sasquachii within the border of our great state (and anywhere else) protected as a Washington State resource and be hereafter, the Official State Monster." The proclamation document compellingly had attached to it "a lock of hair from the right front shoulder of the Sasquatch." The authenticity of said alleged sasquatch hair remains a mystery to this author. As official sounding as Governor Evans' proclamation was, like all ceremonial proclamations made by the Office of the Governor of Washington, it was not legally binding and was "strictly ceremonial."

In early 2017, State Senator Ann Rivers received a handwritten letter from a third-grade student. In the letter, young Caleb expressed his interest in sasquatches and requested that they be recognized as the official "state cryptid" of Washington. Rather than throw the letter away or ignore her young constituent, Senator Rivers instead reacted promptly and introduced Senate Bill 5816 to the state senate on February 15th of 2017. Rivers admitted to being moved by Caleb's letter, saying that his fascination with the legend reminded her of her own two sons when they were his age. SB 5816 would have not only designated the sasquatch species Washington's official state cryptid, but also recognized its "immeasurable contributions to Washington state's cultural heritage and ecosystem." Despite such heartwarming origins and the attention SB 5816 drew, it ultimately failed to come into law. However, the bill was briefly revived in early January 2019 in the form of Senate Bill 5615. Rivers, along with a few of her fellow senators, reintroduced the bill, keeping SB 5816's original language. This attempt would also be unsuccessful and so, for the time being, Washington remains without an official state cryptid.

FRANCISCO ARBENZ

STATE OF WASHINGTON
OFFICE OF THE GOVERNOR

OLYMPIA

DANIEL J. EVANS
GOVERNOR

PROCLAMATION: DESIGNATION OF STATE MONSTER

WHEREAS, recent developments have shown that Washington State has only one true mysterious monster, the Great Sasquatch, and it is endangered of imminent extinction, and

WHEREAS, we are the only state which is able to claim the Sasquatch as our own,

NOW, THEREFORE, I Daniel J. Evans, by virtue and authority vested in me by RCW 00.00.000 do proclaim all Sasquachii within the border of our great state (and anywhere else) protected as a Washington State resource and be hereafter, the Official State Monster.

IN WITNESS WHEREOF, I have caused my machine to forge my signature and have affixed a lock of hair from the right front shoulder of the Sasquatch this twenty-sixth day of August, nineteen hundred and seventy.

Governor Of Washington

S-1505.2

SENATE BILL 5816

State of Washington   65th Legislature   2017 Regular Session

By Senator Rivers

Read first time 02/15/17. Referred to Committee on State Government.

1   AN ACT Relating to designating Sasquatch the official cryptid or
2 crypto-animal of Washington; adding a new section to chapter 1.20
3 RCW; and creating a new section.

4 BE IT ENACTED BY THE LEGISLATURE OF THE STATE OF WASHINGTON:

5   NEW SECTION. **Sec. 1.** The legislature recognizes that Sasquatch
6 has made immeasurable contributions to Washington state's cultural
7 heritage and ecosystem. The state of Washington further recognizes
8 the importance of preserving the legacy of Sasquatch.

9   NEW SECTION. **Sec. 2.** A new section is added to chapter 1.20 RCW
10 to read as follows:
11   The species of cryptid commonly called "Sasquatch" or "Bigfoot"
12 or "Forest Yeti" is hereby designated as the official cryptid of the
13 state of Washington.

--- END ---

FRANCISCO ARBENZ

S-0670.1   _____

SENATE BILL 5615
_____

State of Washington   **66th Legislature**   **2019 Regular Session**

By Senators Rivers, Palumbo, Randall, and Wellman

Read first time 01/25/19.   Referred to Committee on State Government,
Tribal Relations & Elections.

1   AN ACT Relating to designating Sasquatch the official cryptid or
2 crypto-animal of Washington; adding a new section to chapter 1.20
3 RCW; and creating a new section.

4 BE IT ENACTED BY THE LEGISLATURE OF THE STATE OF WASHINGTON:

5   NEW SECTION. **Sec. 1.** The legislature recognizes that Sasquatch
6 has made immeasurable contributions to Washington state's cultural
7 heritage and ecosystem. The state of Washington further recognizes
8 the importance of preserving the legacy of Sasquatch.

9   NEW SECTION. **Sec. 2.** A new section is added to chapter 1.20 RCW
10 to read as follows:
11   The species of cryptid commonly called "Sasquatch" or "Bigfoot"
12 or "Forest Yeti" is hereby designated as the official cryptid of the
13 state of Washington.

--- END ---

30

3

HONORABLE MENTIONS

The following are some monster law related factoids that don't directly relate to monster legislation, but are interesting to learn about, nonetheless.

Texas

COME AND GET ME

Despite Texas sorely lacking any laws or regulations regarding sasquatches, that doesn't mean that there haven't been curious questions posed and answers unearthed regarding the legality of hunting one in the Lone Star State. Back in 2012, a gentleman from Salem, Oregon contacted the Texas Parks and Wildlife Department to inquire as to whether sasquatches were a protected species in Texas. Apparently asking out of concern for the survival of the species in Texas and the lack of protective measures in place to ensure it, the Texas Parks and Wildlife Department's response likely did little to assuage him. David Sinclair, the Department's Chief of Staff responded with an email saying, "if the Commission does not specifically list an indigenous, nongame species, then the species is considered nonprotected nongame wildlife." Mr. Sinclair then concluded, "a nonprotected nongame animal may be hunted on private property with landowner consent by any means, at any time . . . " In other words, since the sasquatch species isn't explicitly listed as a protected species in Texas, it is fair game for all hunters. This wouldn't be the last time the Texas Parks and Wildlife Department commented on the potential for sasquatch hunting. In 2014, game warden Major Larry Young stated, "[w]e don't acknowledge that one exists. But if you wanted to shoot and kill a Bigfoot in the state of Texas, you would just need a hunting license." With hunters armed with both rifles and state agency approval, all sasquatches should tread carefully in the Lone Star State.

Mason County, West Virginia

You may not be familiar with Mason County, West Virginia, unless you're a fan of monster lore. If you are, then you're probably aware that this county is home to the small city of Point Pleasant. For 13 months, from November of 1966 to December of 1967, this sleepy city was terrorized by a large, winged, humanoid creature known colloquially as the Mothman. At least 100 eyewitnesses claimed to have seen the Mothman during this time, and several attempts were made to kill or capture it.

A popular stance taken by skeptics concerning the Mothman was that witnesses were merely spotting an owl or sandhill crane. Strange as these explanations may be, Dr. Robert Smith of West Virginia University's Biology department espoused the latter as a potential explanation for the supposed Mothman. A November 19th, 1966, article from the *Point Pleasant Register* titled "Our Bird Has Law on Its Side" reported how if this were the case, and the Mothman indeed turned out to be a misidentified sandhill crane, then any attempts to kill it would face the brunt of several state and federal laws that protect such migratory birds. The article quotes Deputy Sheriff

Millard Halstead as being all too willing to apprehend anyone "in the TNT area with a loaded gun after dark."

The TNT area he was referring to is an abandoned munitions storage facility consisting of several military bunkers from WWII, and is now known as the McClintic Wildlife Management Area. Many Mothman sightings took place in the TNT area during the 13 months it was seen, during which time would-be Mothman hunters frequented the area and people like Dr. Robert Smith grew concerned for the safety of any misidentified sandhill cranes. Sandhill cranes had a dwindling population east of the Mississippi in the early half of the 20th century but have since recovered greatly and are no longer considered an endangered species, except for two nonmigratory subspecies in Florida and Mississippi. Since the early 2000s, Point Pleasant has hosted a yearly Mothman Festival to celebrate the mysterious creature, and is home to the Mothman Museum as well as a 13-foot-tall statue of the creature. Whether the Mothman truly was a misidentified sandhill crane or not, one thing remains certain - the city of Point Pleasant loves all its winged denizens.

Our 'Bird' Has Law On Its Side

If Mason County's "b i r d" should prove to be a Sand hill Crane, as suggested by Dr Robert Smith of the West Vir ginia University Biology De partment, then the law is on its side to provide protection.

Officials note that migratory birds of all kinds are protected by federal and state wildlife laws.

Millard Halstead, Mason Coun ty Sheriff's Deputy, said Friday, he had been in contact with Dr. Smith and from a compari son of descriptions feels that the "bird man" might be a S a n d h i l l Crane. The bird stands five to six feet tall, has about an 80 - inch wing spread and has patches of red around its eyes.

Halstead said the bird is ex tremely rare, and he under stands there are only 30 of them left in this country.

Sheriff George Johnson said he would arrest any persons caught in the TNT area with a loaded gun after dark. There were earlier reports of armed people roaming the area. John son has asked that residents not harm the bird.

Point Pleasant Register *Nov. 19, 1966 /Photo Courtesy of the Mothman Museum*

New Jersey

The legend of the Jersey Devil, sometimes called the Leeds Devil, is widely known throughout the United States, rivaling cryptozoological legends like Champ and sasquatches. Described as having a horse head, hoofed feet, and a large pair of wings, eyewitnesses have spotted the Jersey Devil since the 1800s and many New Jerseyans are familiar with the associated legend.

Beginning sometime in the 18th century, the legend goes that a woman known as Mother Leeds gave birth to a thirteenth child who she cursed and proclaimed to be the Devil. Once the child was born, it suddenly sprouted wings, transformed into the Jersey Devil we know today, and flew out a window into New Jersey's Pine Barrens. Since then, the legend of the Jersey Devil has captivated the public's imagination, with the well-known hockey team the New Jersey Devils being named after it. But perhaps the Jersey Devil's second biggest claim to fame is becoming the only "official state demon" in the United States. Though it has been echoed by countless online news articles and blogs, is there any truth to this claim?

Research carried out by Link, the official publication of the New

Jersey State Library, determined that the earliest mention of the Jersey Devil being the "official state demon" was in the Wall Street Journal on October 31, 1979, and was later repeated by the New Jersey Public Broadcasting Authority in a documentary sometime later. Both sources cite 1939 as the year in which the Jersey Devil was appointed as official state demon. The Link, however, was unable to find any laws from 1939 that appointed the Jersey Devil as such. Their team was able to further track down the 1939 claim to a book published that year titled *New Jersey: A guide to its Present and Past.* The book's chapter titled "Folklore and Folkways" states that, "by default, the title of official State demon has rested for nearly a century with the Leeds Devil." However, the Link team went on to discredit the validity of this book as they found that it also claimed the Jersey Devil was working on his "doctorate from the University of Hell"... among other outlandish claims. The Link's official publication concludes, "the idea that the legendary Jersey Devil is the official state demon of New Jersey is itself an urban legend." Nevertheless, the legend of the Jersey Devil lives on in the hearts and minds of countless New Jerseyans, and possibly in the vast wilderness of the Pine Barrens.

Monster Law Map

REFERENCES

"Agriculture." *Bellingham Whatcom County Tourism,* Drozian Webworks, https://www.bellingham.org/agricultural. Accessed 13 September 2023.

"All About Birds: Sandhill Crane: Range Map." *The Cornell Lab,* Cornell University, https://www.allaboutbirds.org/guide/Sandhill_Crane/maps-range. Accessed 13 September 2023.

Barker, Larry. "Taxpayers on the hook for UNM Bigfoot expedition." *KRQE News,* Nexstar Media Inc., 17 May 2022, https://www.krqe.com/news/taxpayers-on-the-hook-for-unm-bigfoot-expedition/. Accessed 13 September 2023.

Buchiere, Steve. "City OKs Linden Street closures, with changes." *Finger Lakes Times,* 3 March 2017, https://www.fltimes.com/news/city-oks-linden-street-closures-with-changes/article_30cf51d0-001d-11e7-8cda-97e499f6c4c1.html. Accessed 13 September 2023.

"Champ, the Lake Champlain Monster." *Lake Champlain Region,* https://www.lakechamplainregion.com/heritage/champ. Accessed 13 September 2023.

"Christopher Dyer." *The University of New Mexico – Gallup, https://gallup.unm.edu/diversity/speakers/christopher-dyer.html.* Accessed 13 September 2023.

Corrigan, Richard. "Seneca Lake Fishing: Complete Angler's Guide." *Best Fishing in America,* https://www.bestfishinginamerica.com/new-york-seneca-lake-fishing.html. Accessed 13 September 2023.

Department of Environmental Conservation. "Seneca Lake." *New York State,* https://www.dec.ny.gov/outdoor/25574.html. Accessed 13 September 2023.

"Douglas D. Osheroff – Facts." *The Nobel Prize,* Nobel Prize Outreach AB 2023, 7 December 1996, https://www.nobelprize.org/prizes/physics/1996/osheroff/lecture/. Accessed 13 September 2023.

"Does New Jersey Have an Official Demon?" *New Jersey State Library,* The Newsletter for State Employees, www.njstatelib.org. Accessed 13 September 2023.

"Faculty: Professors." *Idaho State University,* https://www.isu.edu/biology/people/faculty---professors/jeffrey-meldrum/. Accessed 13 September 2023.

Figura, David. "Upstate NY community names Sasquatch its 'official animal'." *NYup.com,* Advance Local Media LLC, 5 July 2018, https://www.newyorkupstate.com/outdoors/2018/07/upstate_ny_community_names_sasquatch_its_official_animal.html. Accessed 13 September 2023.

Gebhardt, Erika. "Students Ask Grays Harbor Commissioners for Protections for the Elusive Sasquatch Population." *The Chronicle,* 20 April 2022, https://www.chronline.com/stories/students-ask-grays-harbor-commissioners-for-protections-for-the-elusive-sasquatch-population,289703. Accessed 13 September 2023.

"Grays Harbor designated as a "Sasquatch protection and refuge area"." *KXRO News*

Radio, 6 April 2022, *https://www.kxro.com/grays-harbor-designated-as-a-sasquatch-protection-and-refuge-area/*. Accessed 13 September 2023.

Grundhauser, Eric. "Ape Canyon: Cougar, Washington." *Atlas Obscura*, 7 November 2014, https://www.atlasobscura.com/places/ape-canyon. Accessed 13 September 2023.

Gribble, Rachel. "Bigfoot expedition inspires ban on state-funded searches for mythical creatures." *NBC4i.com*. Nexstar Media Inc., 12 February 2017, https://www.nbc4i.com/news/bigfoot-expedition-inspires-ban-on-state-funded-searches-for-mythical-creatures/. Accessed 13 September 2023.

Henry, Terrence. "Is It Legal to Kill Bigfoot in Texas?." *State Impact*, 10 May 2012, https://stateimpact.npr.org/texas/2012/05/10/is-it-legal-to-kill-bigfoot-in-texas/. Accessed 13 September 2023.

Hlavaty, Craig. "PETA says no to Bigfoot hunting." *CHRON,* Hearst Newspapers, LLC, 29 January 2014, https://www.chron.com/news/strange-weird/article/PETA-says-no-to-Bigfoot-hunting-5185492.php. Accessed 13 September 2023.

"Home: Welcome to Whitehall, New York online!." *Town and Village of Whitehall, New York*, http://www.whitehallny.org/. Accessed 13 September 2023.

"Historic Marker: Champy." *William G. Pomeroy Foundation*, https://www.wgpfoundation.org/historic-markers/10700-2/. Accessed 13 September 2023.

Hunter, Jeff. "Whitehall names Sasquatch its official animal." *News10.com*, Your Local News Leader, 5 July 2018, https://www.news10.com/news/local-news/whitehall-names-sasquatch-its-official-animal/#:~:text=Bigfoot%20sightings%20-date%20back%20to%20the%20Iroquois%20and,in%20the%20early%20-part%20of%20the%2021st%20Century. Accessed 13 September 2023.

Manz, William H. *Gibson's New York Legal Research Guide*. Buffalo, New York, William S. Hein & Co., 10 December 2004

Metrick, Becky. "Oklahoma lawmaker files bill to create 'Bigfoot hunting season'." *PENN LIVE*, Advance Local Media LLC., 22 January 2021, https://www.pennlive.com/news/2021/01/oklahoma-lawmaker-files-bill-to-create-bigfoot-hunting-season.html#:~:text=An%20Oklahoma%20State%20Representative%20-filed%20a%20bill%20to,and%20any%20%E2%80%9Cnecessary%20specif-ic%20hunting%20licenses%20and%20fees.%E2%80%9D. Accessed 13 September 2023.

Mitchell, Josh. "Woman believes she has sonar images of Champ: Champ said to be lake monster in Lake Champlain." *NBC5 News*, Hearst Television Inc., 25 August 2019, https://www.mynbc5.com/article/woman-believes-she-has-sonar-images-of-champ/28810114. Accessed 13 September 2023.

Moriah Chamber of Commerce. "Champ Day: The Lake Champlain Monster Festival." *Port Henry-Moriah*, 5 August 2023, https://www.porthenrymoriah.com/events-0. Accessed 13 September 2023.

"Mothman Statue: Point Pleasant, West Virginia." *RoadsideAmerica.com*, https://www.roadsideamerica.com/story/12036. Accessed 13 September 2023.

News, KGW. "KGW Archive: 1971 Washington Sasquatch report." *You Tube*, 10 July 2019, https://www.youtube.com/watch?v=4XmPP3iktPE. Accessed 13 September 2023.

Poisuo, Pauli. "The Jersey Devil Might Actually Have Existed. Here's Why." *GRUNG*, 21 December 2020, https://www.grunge.com/229558/the-jersey-devil-might-actually-have-existed-heres-why/. Accessed 13 September 2023.

Radford, Benjamin. "Champ: America's Loch Ness Monster." *Live Science*, Future US, Inc., 30 May 2013, https://www.livescience.com/37012-lake-champlain-monster.html. Accessed 13 September 2023.

"Request a ceremonial proclamation, greeting or letter." *WA.gov*, Office of Governor Jay Inslee, https://governor.wa.gov/contacting-governor/requests-invites/request-ceremonial-proclamation-greeting-or-letter. Accessed 13 September 2023.

"Sandhill Crane." *American Bird Conservancy*, https://abcbirds.org/bird/sandhill-crane/. Accessed 13 September 2023.

"Sandhill Crane." *The Nature Conservancy*, 16 June 2021, https://www.nature.org/en-us/get-involved/how-to-help/animals-we-protect/sandhill-crane/. Accessed 13 September 2023.

Scott, Douglas. "Five Places in Aberdeen to Find the Spirit of Kurt Cobain." *Grays-Harbor Talk*, 28 April 2017, https://www.graysharbortalk.com/2017/04/28/five-places-in-aberdeen-to-find-the-spirit-of-kurt-cobain/. Accessed 13 September 2023.

Seneca County Historian Walter Gable. "The Sea Serpent of Seneca Lake." *Seneca County, New York*, October 2009, https://co.seneca.ny.us/wp-content/uploads/2020/01/The-Sea-Serpent-of-Seneca-Lake-ADA.pdf. Accessed 13 September 2023.

Staff, Live Science. "Want to Shoot Bigfoot? It's Legal in Texas." *Live Science*, 11 May 2012, https://www.livescience.com/20248-shooting-bigfoot-legal-texas.html. Accessed 13 September 2023.

"The Jersey Devil and Folklore." *Pinelands Preservation Alliance*, https://pinelandsalliance.org/learn-about-the-pinelands/pinelands-history-and-culture/the-jersey-devil-and-folklore/. Accessed 13 September 2023.

Thomas, Nicki. "Sasquatch." *The Canadian Encyclopedia*, *Historica Canada*, 26 January 2018, www.thecanadianencyclopedia.ca/en/article/sasquatch. Accessed 13 September 2023.

"TNT Area: Point Pleasant, West Virginia." *Atlas Obscura*, 6 June 2009, https://www.atlasobscura.com/places/tnt-area. Accessed 13 September 2023.

Tung, Angela. "The mysterious origins of the Jersey Devil." *The Week*, Future US, Inc., 8 January 2015, https://theweek.com/articles/442631/mysterious-origins-jersey-devil. Accessed 13 September 2023.

U.S. Board on Geographic Names (BGN). "Approved Sq_ replacement names." *USGS: Science for a Changing World*, esri, 13 January 2023, https://edits.nationalmap.gov/apps/gaz-domestic/public/all-official-sq-names. Accessed 13 September 2023.

"United States: Washington." *The Big Foot Field Researchers Organization*, 2022, https://www.bfro.net/GDB/state_listing.asp?state=wa. Accessed 13 September 2023.

Wenzelburger, Jared. "Thanks to Fifth Graders, Bigfoot Protections Grow in Washington." *The chronicle*, 28 April 2023, https://www.chronline.com/stories/thanks-to-fifth-graders-bigfoot-protections-grow-in-washington,318282. Accessed 13 September 2023.

ABOUT THE AUTHOR

A Native New Yorker, Francisco grew up in Brooklyn and Staten Island before moving to upstate New York to study both History and Law. He received a BA in History from SUNY New Paltz in 2021 and a Juris Doctor from Albany Law School in 2024. MONSTER LAW is his latest attempt at blending both of his lifelong interests in law and all things strange.

AFTERWORD

Go to hangaɪpublishing.com to learn more about the Authors and stay up to date with their newest releases.

www.ingramcontent.com/pod-product-compliance
Lightning Source LLC
Chambersburg PA
CBHW061325120626
46546CB00007B/2680